PRAYER THAT WILL AWAKEN AMERICA AND THE WORLD!

A BIBLICAL GUIDE TO EFFECTIVE PRAYER IN THE TIME OF COVID-19, AND BEYOND!

PASTOR DANIEL CASTILLO, M.DIV.

WESTBOW
PRESS®
A DIVISION OF THOMAS NELSON
& ZONDERVAN

WestBow Press books may be ordered through booksellers or by contacting:

WestBow Press
A Division of Thomas Nelson & Zondervan
1663 Liberty Drive
Bloomington, IN 47403
www.westbowpress.com
1 (866) 928-1240

ISBN: 978-1-6642-0548-2 (sc)
ISBN: 978-1-6642-0550-5 (hc)
ISBN: 978-1-6642-0549-9 (e)

Library of Congress Control Number: 2020917594

Print information available on the last page.

WestBow Press rev. date: 09/30/2020

I dedicate this book to my wife, Pastor Yvonne Castillo, who through her prayer life has shown me the power of sincere and intense prayer to our Lord, and the miracles He gives as answers. I also thank her for her partnership in ministry experiences that have prepared me to write this book. I also dedicate it to my mother Ophelia, who as a godly mother, has prayed for her family, for me, and my ministry throughout her life. Finally, I dedicate it to the encouragement of our friend, apostle Jackie London, of Pillar of Fire Worship Center, Warsaw, North Carolina, who earlier this year prophesied that I would persevere until I wrote this book!

CONTENTS

CHAPTER 1

"IF MY PEOPLE"

CHAPTER OVERVIEW

In this day of COVID-19 and other disasters, many activities in our lives may be restricted but our faith is not! We will receive deliverance from this pandemic, and other corporate disasters we face, by praying united prayers of repentance as the body of Christ. These prayers will also bring revival to the Church and awakening to God in America and the world! That overcoming this pandemic and other nationwide or worldwide disasters would have anything to do with sin and repentance may be jarring, but God does use tragedy or disaster to refocus our lives, realign us, return us to a needed dependence on Him and bring spiritual blessing!

UNITED, HUMBLE PRAYER, BECAUSE OF SIN

"Then the Lord appeared to Solomon by night, and said to him: I have heard your prayer, and have chosen this place for Myself as a house of sacrifice. When I shut up heaven and there is no rain or command the locusts to devour the land,

or send pestilence among My people, 'If My people, who are called by My name will humble themselves, and pray and seek My face, and turn from their wicked ways, then I will hear from heaven, and will forgive their sin and heal their land.'" (2 Chronicles 7:12—14)

God spoke these words to Solomon, king of Israel, as part of His response to Solomon's prayer for His blessing on the temple Solomon had built, when it was being dedicated. God's intention was that Solomon share these words with the people of Israel, who were to follow these instructions and come to the temple to cry out for God's mercy, when God was forced to discipline them. God's people today don't have a structural temple building on earth, but the Bible says to the Church of Jesus Christ that we ourselves are His temple, His dwelling place, through His Holy Spirit, so these instructions still apply, as we are to pray from the sites of our "temples."

"Or do you not know that your body is the temple of the Holy Spirit who is in you, whom you have from God, and you are not your own? For you were bought at a price; therefore glorify God in your body and in your spirit, which are God's." (1 Corinthians 6:19, 20)

God's words in 2 Chronicles 7:12-14 say that God's way for stopping a corporate disaster He has "sent" (v. 13), or it could also be said, "allowed," such as the COVID-19 pestilence, is simple, yet profound: it is united, humble prayer among His people. Yes, the pandemic originated in China, but God allowed this unprecedented disaster to spread worldwide. Why? Because of sin; sin in the Church and sin in the world. To many, this may seem jarring, but doesn't God regularly use personal tragedy or corporate disasters as a way to refocus our lives, realign them, and return to a needed repentance and dependence on Him? As with ancient Israel, God wants us to take our sin seriously and repent of it (turn from our wicked ways), because sin is much more dangerous for us than a pandemic, since it causes consequences in our lives, in our loved ones' lives, in the lives of others, in our nation and world, and can even send us to hell forever. God allows disaster so we will re-examine our lives, stop being lukewarm about sin, escape sin's judgment, commit or recommit ourselves to Him, live faithful lives, and have a future in heaven!

When our Lord first spoke these words in 2 Chronicles 7:12-14, His people were the twelve tribes of Israel. Today, along with God's historic people Israel, God's people include the Church of the Lord Jesus Christ. To stop widespread disaster, such as pestilence, our Lord tells His people to humbly pray as a united people. Often it is hard to lay down our pride and pray, even with other Christians with whom we agree about the essentials of the faith, because we have had differences or disagreements with them in the past, because we disagree with them regarding lesser points in the faith or because they attend other churches.

That was the reality among the 12 tribes. They had a history of disagreements with each other about various issues, and pride about these disagreements, but they were still one people. God told them that if they would come to the temple and pray together in the face of disaster, He would answer and deliver them! Because of the seriousness of COVID-19, and other situations we all face or may face in the future, the Body of Christ needs to lay aside our pride and pray with each other for God's mercy and deliverance!

- *As we face of COVID-19, we Christians can pray together for an end to this pandemic and other disasters on our phones and through social media, at home with our spouses and families, or agreeing with prayers in Christian publications, Christian radio and Christian T.V., until the day we can again pray in person. We can stop this pandemic, and any other disaster we are facing, by praying united prayers of repentance. These prayers will also bring revival to the Church and awakening to God in America and the world!*

INTENSE, SINCERE, AND REPENTANT PRAYER

When faced with a widespread disaster, our Lord also tells us in 2 Chronicles 7:14, that we are to "seek His face." "Seeking His face" is prayer that is so intense, sincere and repentant that we come face-to-face with God. Jacob sought the face of God when he prayed to God the night before facing an uncertain meeting with his stronger and still resentful brother Esau, whom Jacob tricked, along with his mother Rebekah, of his blessing and birthright many years before (See Genesis 26:34—27:1—45. Although God did want the blessing and birthright for Jacob instead of Esau, God could have worked this out for Jacob in another way.). This meeting could have cost Jacob his life. Esau was coming to meet Jacob with four hundred men on horseback, a sign that after all these years, he was still angry with and suspicious of him. During Jacob's prayer, recorded in Genesis 32:24—32, the Bible says that Jacob wrestled with a Man all night, a Man who renamed him "Israel," for the Man said, "you have struggled with God and with men, and have prevailed" (The name "Israel" means "struggles with God."). This Man, who was really the Lord, also blessed Jacob.

Jacob called the place of this encounter "Peniel," meaning "the face of God," for he said, "...I have seen God face to face, and my life is preserved." (Genesis 32:30b) He meant that as a sinner, despite meeting with a holy God "face to face," God allowed him to live. During his prayer, Jacob saw himself as God saw him and repented of his underhanded and manipulative ways. In the morning, Jacob's life was also preserved when he met Esau, who by then was inexplicably gracious toward him, a brother whose heart God had surely melted overnight in answer to Jacob's intense, sincere, and repentant prayer.

During his intense all-night prayer, Jacob would not let go of the Lord as he wrestled with Him. The Lord could have easily overpowered Jacob at any time, but He showed him that He was willing to be held onto by Jacob, as long as he was sincere, intense, and repentant in seeking His blessing. So that Jacob would "let Him go," the Bible says that our Lord "touched the socket of his hip." (Genesis 32:25) Jacob's hip was knocked out of joint, and afterward, he would always walk with a limp. This was a reminder to Jacob that although God answered his prayer, He did so only when Jacob humbled himself, and was intensely, sincerely, and repentantly holding on to Him. In the same way, God wants to answer our prayers, but will do so only when we intensely, sincerely and repentantly humble ourselves when asking for His help.

When we as God's people pray in the face of disaster, we need to pray repentant prayers, because it is sin in the Church and in the world that has brought God's judgment. Repentance involves not only confessing sin, but turning away from it ("turning from our wicked ways," 2 Chronicles 7:14).

We know that there is sin in the world, but there is also sin in the Church, though it is often "under wraps." Furthermore, the Church at times sins by being complicit with sin, that is, by ignoring it, not calling it out prophetically, because we do not want to be persecuted for speaking out or are even desensitized to certain sins. Before this pandemic, many were joyfully celebrating laws passed by some state legislatures in the United States, including New York, permitting abortion until the time of birth in the name of "women's rights." Obedient Christians should have been calling out this sin prophetically. Some were, but how many? How many Christians now see abortion as a "woman's right" or don't want to speak out against it and be attacked? Strangely, New York City, in New York state, eventually became the worldwide epicenter of this terrible pandemic.

INTERCESSORY AND IDENTIFICATIONAL PRAYER

When God's people face disaster, we not only need to repent "and turn from our wicked ways," but also pray intercessory prayers for the world, as did our Lord Jesus, the apostle Paul and others in the Bible. Intercessory prayers are prayers to God on behalf of others, in this case, that God would have mercy on the world in the face of this pandemic.

In John 12:32, 33, our Lord Jesus spoke about what was surely the greatest intercessory prayer of His heart, "And I, if I am lifted up from the earth (If I be lifted up on a cross), will draw all peoples to Myself. This He said, signifying by what death He would die." In Luke 23:34, our Lord Jesus, while He was in the very act of being crucified, prayed an intercessory prayer for His tormentors, "Father, forgive them, for they do not know what they do."

In 1st Timothy 2:1—4, the apostle Paul tells us, "Therefore I exhort first of all that supplications, prayers, intercessions, and giving of thanks be made for all men, for kings and all who are in authority, that we may lead a quiet and peaceable life in all godliness and reverence. For this is good and acceptable in the sight of God our Savior, who desires all men to be saved and come to the knowledge of the truth."

Intercessory prayer is powerful when we love the world enough to identify with its sins, praying identificational prayers, as if we ourselves were committing or had committed those sins. Although they themselves had not sinned, the prophet Daniel, in Daniel 9, and the Jewish leader Nehemiah, in Nehemiah 1:4—11, prayed on behalf of the people of Israel who had lived in sin and suffered disaster because of it, identifying with their sin, and asking for God's forgiveness. God answered both of these prayers mightily, by restoring the people of Israel to their land, after He had allowed them to be expelled from it because of their sin, and helping them rebuild the walls of Jerusalem, their capital city, which He had allowed to be destroyed by an enemy because of their sin.

CHAPTER 2

A QUESTION AND A PROPHECY!

A QUESTION

One of the questions some in the Church have asked about the COVID-19 pandemic was why the Church hadn't heard from God that this pestilence was coming. After all, in the Bible, the principle is clear:

"Surely the Lord does nothing unless He reveals His secret to His servants the prophets." (Amos 3:7)

AND A PROPHECY TO THE LIKELIEST ONES!

But the Lord <u>had</u> spoken! And He had spoken to the likeliest ones to be His mouthpieces about this plague! We just didn't know it!

PASTOR DAVID WILKERSON

God first spoke to the one who for years had most loved, with the precious love of God, the place which was to be the epicenter of this pandemic: New York City! He spoke to David Wilkerson, who as a lone, brave young man, boldly preached to the fierce gangs on the streets of New York City, afterward writing a well-known book about his experiences, a story which was also told on film, <u>The Cross and the Switchblade</u>,[1] featuring his most famous convert, gang leader Nicky Cruz, who himself became an evangelist! Our Lord spoke to David Wilkerson, founder of the effective, Christ-centered addiction recovery ministry, "Teen Challenge," which later became "Adult and Teen Challenge," that has saved, delivered and transformed many lives nationwide and worldwide with the love of God and biblical principles! He spoke to David Wilkerson, founder of the non-denominational Times Square Church, that he began in 1987 to reach New York City with the love of Jesus Christ, a ministry which has inspired others to do the same! Pastor David Wilkerson passed away in a traffic accident in 2011.

THE PROPHECY!

In 1986, our Lord gave the following prophecy to David Wilkerson: **"I see a plague coming on the world and the bars, church and government shut down. The plague will hit New York City and shake it like it has never been shaken. The plague is going to force prayerless Believers into radical prayer, into their Bibles, and repentance will be the cry from true men of God in the**

pulpit. And out of it will come a Third Great Awakening that will sweep America and the world." [2]

PASTOR MIKE EVANS

This prophecy was first delivered by Pastor David Wilkerson to Dr. Michael David Evans, an American Jewish Christian who has probably loved the nation of Israel as much or more than any other American. Dr. Evans, a converted Jew, a long-time friend of Israel, a friend of Israel's prime ministers and leaders, a journalist and author of significant books about the Middle East and Christian end-times prophecy, among other activities, has established The Friends of Zion Museum in Jerusalem and is founder of The Jerusalem Prayer Team, an organization participated-in by millions of Christians worldwide. Recently, Dr. Evans has written an important book about this prophecy: A Great Awakening is Coming.[3] God had Pastor Wilkerson speak this prophecy not only to a Jew (just as He spoke the words in 2 Chronicles 2:12—14 to Jewish King Solomon and the Jewish people), but to the person, because of his life and credentials, most likely to be believed by the Church worldwide, Dr. Michael Evans. As Dr. Evans tells it, in 1986, as he was having lunch with David Wilkerson at the Embassy Suites Hotel near the Dallas-Fort Worth International Airport, he wrote this prophecy as it was spoken to him by his friend on piece of paper. Dr. Evans placed the prophecy in the Bible he was using at the time. 34 years later, in 2020, in the early stages of the COVID-19 pandemic in the United States, Dr. Evans recalled the prophecy, reached for his old Bible and the paper on which it was written fell out! [4]

A fearsome plague has come upon the world. The bars and many other establishments, such as restaurants and many small businesses, the government and the Church in the United States and in many places in the world, have shut down. New York City, the largest city in the United States, has been the city most shaken by this pandemic, not only in the United States but in the world! Will a Third Great Awakening come out of this? Only if believers, including many prayerless believers radically pray, get into their Bibles and repent, and only if repentance is the cry from America's pulpits! We need revival in the Church and awakening in the world even more than we need for this pandemic and other corporate disasters to go away, as the stakes for unrepentant people are eternal!

CHAPTER 3

HISTORIC REVIVALS AND AWAKENINGS

CHAPTER OVERVIEW

Revival is "the coming to life" of the Church, while Awakening is "the coming to life" of the world. Revival comes through a move of the Holy Spirit inspiring radical prayer and repentance in the Church, which then "wakes the world up" to God. This move of the Holy Spirit can also involve a call for the Church to pray intercessory prayers to stop disasters facing a nation or the world.

THE HEALING OF AMERICA AND ALL LANDS

Pastor Wilkerson's prophecy tells us that COVID-19 will force prayerless believers into radical prayer and Bible study. As a result of these prayers and study, anointed preaching about repentance will come from America's churches, which will result in widespread repentance across America and in the world—a Third Great Awakening! God wants prayer, because prophecy, even one like this is not automatically fulfilled. It must be "prayed-in!" As well-known revivalist Lou Engle says, "Prophecies are an invitation to intercession!" [5]

The importance of "praying-in" Pastor David Wilkerson's prophecy with "radical prayer" for repentance has become even more pressing as the COVID-19 disaster has become just the first of 3 disasters that have come upon contemporary America, the second being America's participation in worldwide economic disaster caused by the virus, and the third, political upheaval and widespread lawlessness.

What is often misunderstood in America is that we do not have just a political problem. We have a spiritual problem. The deep division in American society is not just political, but between those who believe in God, respect biblical principles, want live by them and desire governance to be based on them, and those who do not or are not concerned about these matters. It is people who are "awakened" to their need of salvation through Jesus Christ and are "awakened" to obey His Lordship, who will elect political leaders who believe in the God of the Bible and apply biblical principles to governance, as the Declaration of Independence and the U.S. Constitution intended. John Adams, the second president of the United States, once declared:

"Our Constitution was made only for a moral and religious people. It is wholly inadequate to the government of any other." [6]

Religious pilgrims who first came to America's shores in the early 1600s, such as Puritan John Winthrop, desired this land to be "a city on a hill," [7] as spoken of by Jesus in His "Sermon on the Mount" (Matthew 5-7), a land that would live in the light of the Gospel of Jesus Christ, and shine the truth of that Gospel to the nations:

"You are the light of the world. A city that is set on a hill cannot be hidden. Nor do they light a lamp and put it under a basket, but on a lampstand, and it gives light to all who are in the house. Let your light so shine before men that they may see your good works and glorify your Father in heaven." (Matthew 5:14, 15)

"THE CURE OF ALL ILLS"

When deep repentance comes to the Church, society will take notice and "awaken" to the Church's message about repentance, forgiveness by God through Jesus Christ and the need for the spiritual transformation of society! In The Cure of all Ills, [8] an incisive book about the history of American religious revivals, author Mary Stuart-Relfe communicates this as her main point: that revival has always been "the cure of all ills" for American society, and by extension, I would add, "the cure of all ills" for societies worldwide.

She details the terrible decay of American society in the years before the Revolutionary War (broken marriages and family life, the dreadful effects of fatherlessness, wanton disrespect for college professors and lawlessness by young people in America's colleges, and widespread alcoholism and drug abuse by American colonists) (Sound familiar? America has been there before!). This was only reversed by prayer, the preaching of repentance by pastors such as Johnathan Edwards (whose most famous sermon was "Sinners in the Hands of an Angry God"), the preaching of repentance by open-air evangelists such as Englishman George Whitfield, and repentance that followed. She explains that this repentance and revival resulted in The First Great Awakening, and that this awakening prepared leaders of the American Revolution to firmly establish the new American nation on Judeo-Christian values.

Mrs. Stuart-Relfe goes on to describe the lawlessness of the American frontier in the early 1800s (the frontier at the time was the American Midsouth), and how its people's wild and corrupt living was only tamed by The Second Great Awakening, a move of God started by prayer, strong preaching about repentance on the frontier by preachers such as Peter Cartwright and Timothy Dwight, and repentance by many at outdoor, days-long, interdenominational camp meetings, bringing revival to the Church and new order and civility to the nation.

She also explains how in 1857, revival in the Church and awakening in society began through the efforts of a young, godly, New York businessman and missionary to immigrants, Jeremiah Lanphier, who began prayer meetings for repentance in New York City businesses at lunch time, which ignited united prayer meetings in the nation's churches. This brought the message of repentance to the nation, changing it and spiritually preparing many men from the North who would later be called upon to die in the Civil War.

IF OUR FOUNDATIONS ARE DESTROYED

"If the foundations are destroyed, what can the righteous do? The Lord is in His holy temple. The Lord's throne is in heaven; His eyes behold, His eyelids test the sons of men. The Lord tests the righteous, but the wicked and the one who loves violence His soul hates. . . . For the Lord is righteous, He loves righteousness; His countenance beholds the upright." (Psalm 11:3—5, 7)

America is in danger of losing its spiritual and moral foundations—its Judeo-Christian values. What can the righteous do? The greatest thing they can do is pray! That is what the psalmist is doing! Why? Because the Lord is ultimately in control. He is still on His throne. He is testing the righteous to see if they will have faith in Him in the midst of this spiritual battle! He is testing the righteous to see if they are truly repentant and will cry out for repentance in the body of Christ and repentance in the world! The Lord is holy and at times like these He sees the anguish of the righteous. If we, like Jacob, are repentant and want His blessing bad enough, He will give it to us! He can turn everything around with a mighty revival of repentance in the Church and a nationwide and worldwide awakening to Jesus Christ! He has done so before when His people have cried out at the lowest points in American and world history and He can do it again!

MORE "MOVES OF GOD"

Furthermore, historians have clearly linked Reform Movements in American society in the 1800s to Christian revivals which occurred at that time, revivals led by Evangelists like the godly lawyer-turned-preacher Charles Finney, and others. These Reform movements included the influential Abolitionist Movement, which led to the Civil War and the freeing of America's slaves, the Women's Suffrage Movement, which led to women's voting rights, and the Social Gospel Movement, whose reforms did much to improve the living and working conditions of America's poor working class. [9]

In the late 19th and early 20th centuries, revival in both American and English churches came about through the devout prayers and preaching of Chicago shoe salesman-turned-evangelist D.L. Moody. At this time, the evangelistic, prophetic and healing ministries of English plumber-turned-evangelist Smith Wigglesworth, American homemaker-turned-evangelist Maria Woodworth-Etter, and Canadian-American healing evangelist John G. Lake, among others, also brought revival. It is said that Maria Woodworth-Etter had such an anointing in the Holy Spirit, that the Spirit would fall in power for repentance not only upon those who heard her, but upon people in homes in regions she merely visited!

A prayer movement of repentance in Los Angeles area churches at the end of the 19th and the beginning of the 20th century, spearheaded by devoted evangelist and intercessor Frank

Bartleman, led to the great Azusa Street Revival and its many conversions, notable healings, and frequent experiences of the visible glory of God, in meetings held in a horse stable-converted into a church! This revival, led by the humble, prayerful, black evangelist and pastor William Seymour, brought about explosive, worldwide Church growth and societal change through those who visited the worship, prayer and healing services at Azusa Street and took the Holy Spirit's power to the rest of America and the world! Several Pentecostal denominations trace their beginnings to Azusa Street, and it has been said that upwards of 750 million people and counting have come to faith in Jesus Christ because of this significant revival!

The great Tent Healing Revivals of the 1940s and 50s, pioneered by Evangelists such as Oral Roberts and William Branham, the rise of the Rev. Billy Graham's influential worldwide evangelistic ministry begun in the same period, the worldwide Charismatic Renewal in mainstream Protestant and Roman Catholic churches sprouting in the late 1960s, the rise of the Jesus Movement in America and the Calvary Chapel Movement from within the counterculture of the 1960s and 70s, the 1990s Toronto Vineyard Blessing, the 1990s Brownsville Assembly of God Pensacola Outpouring, and the 2008 Lakeland, Florida, Revival, broadcast worldwide, among others, brought many to repentance and faith in Jesus Christ, a deep experience with the ministry and power of the Holy Spirit and a new understanding of the loving "Father Heart" of God!

Throughout history, there have been great revivals, awakenings and transformations in the Church and society in others lands as well, all birthed in radical prayers of repentance: from the great Protestant Reformation in Europe in the 16th and 17th centuries, the Moravian prayer and missionary movement in the 18th century, the evangelical revivals and missionary movements in England in the 18th and 19th centuries, and great revivals and awakenings in English Wales, Korea, China, India, the Scottish Hebrides Islands, Africa and Central and South America from the late 19th through the 20th centuries. Many of these later revivals and awakenings have had their genesis in American revivals, awakenings, and mission work, because the greatest reason America was created by God was for it to be the key nation in bringing the Gospel of Jesus Christ to the nations!

CHAPTER 4

RADICAL, UNITED PRAYER! CURRENT REVELATIONS ABOUT REVIVAL AND AWAKENING!

CHAPTER OVERVIEW

We in America need healing, as spoken of in 2 Chronicles 7:13, 14, not only from a terrible pandemic and other disasters, but from a greater, spiritual disease: sin and the devastation it causes.

RADICAL, UNITED PRAYER!

Why are America and the world experiencing a prolonged, lengthy pandemic that has brought deepening economic depression and social distress? Why have racial tensions morphed into radical political protests, widespread rioting, looting, lawlessness and more political upheaval? Can it be because our Lord is waiting for radical prayer to rise up in His Church? We in America and the world need healing, as spoken of in 2 Chronicles 7:14, not just from a terrible pandemic, but from a greater, spiritual disease: sin and the devastation it causes.

"If My people, who are called by My name will humble themselves, and pray and seek My face, and turn from their wicked ways, then I will hear from heaven, and will forgive their sin and heal their land.'" (2 Chronicles 7:14)

Today, we need to pray radically to bring-in this physical and spiritual healing, as a united Church of Jesus Christ! This may well bring about the last great awakening and harvest of souls before the second coming of our Lord Jesus Christ, as prophesied in the Old Testament Books of Hosea, Joel and the New Testament Book of Acts:

"Come, and let us return to the Lord; for He has torn, but He will heal us; He has stricken, but He will bind us up. After two days He will revive us; on the third day He will raise us up, that we may live in his sight. Let us know, let us pursue the knowledge of the Lord, His going forth is established as the morning; He will come to us like the rain, like the latter and former rain to the earth." (Hosea 6:1—3)

"And it shall come to pass afterward that I will pour out My Spirit on all flesh; Your sons and your daughters shall prophesy, your old men shall dream dreams, your young men shall see visions. And also on My menservants and My maidservants I will pour out My Spirit in those days. And I will show wonders in the heavens and in the earth: Blood and fire and pillars of smoke. The sun shall be turned into

darkness and the moon into blood, before the coming of the great and awesome day of the Lord. And it shall come to pass that whoever calls on the name of the Lord shall be saved. . . . " (Joel 2:28—32a)

"But those things which God foretold by the mouth of all His prophets, that the Christ would suffer, He has thus fulfilled. Repent therefore and be converted, that your sins may be blotted out, so that times of refreshing may come from the presence of the Lord, and that He may send Jesus Christ, who was preached to you before, whom heaven must receive until the times of restoration of all things, which God has spoken by the mouth of all His holy prophets since the world began." (Acts 4:18—21)

The simple power of radical, united, repentant prayer by God's people to move the hand of God and bring healing in the face of disaster, revival in the Church and awakening in society, should no longer be overlooked by God's people!

CURRENT REVELATIONS ABOUT REVIVAL AND AWAKENING!

My wife Yvonne and I attended the "Summer of Glory Conference" held June 20-23, 2019, sponsored by David Herzog Ministries in Phoenix, AZ. [10] My wife especially went for the worship and experience of the glory, and I, especially to hear revivalist Lou Engle, the father of the modern-day Azusa Street Prayer Movement and founder of The Call, a ministry of Church-wide prayer and evangelism for the end-time harvest. Lou is known to have a powerful prophetic anointing, so I was keenly interested in what he had to say about a coming revival and awakening. I was not disappointed in what God had to say through this raspy, prayerful, direct preacher of holiness and revival!

In front of us was a modern-day Frank Bartleman. Bartleman, as previously mentioned, was the man who, in the Los Angeles area at the turn of the 20th century, at high personal cost, sacrificed and prayed for the coming of revival, seeing it come in a truly powerful way at Azusa Street! Now, we were hearing from a man who for years has prayed for a revival that would eclipse the power of Azusa Street, and bring-in the final end-time harvest! In fact, one of Lou's friends once had a dream in which he saw the front cover of Frank Bartleman's book about the Azusa Street Revival, Azusa Street,[11] opened. Inside the front cover was a photo of Frank Bartleman, that in the dream transformed itself into a photo of Lou Engle, confirming Lou's call to pray for a second Azusa Street! [12]

In his message at this conference, Lou's first call was to repentance and then to unity in the body of Christ! He spoke of idols in his life that God had called him to give up in his quest for revival. For example, with the agreement of his family, he sold the family's 1.3 million-dollar home, a gift from one of his supporters, to invest the money into the ministry for revival and awakening, especially through stadium evangelism. [13]

When sharing about unity, Lou recounted that one of his friends once called him about a dream he had a night before. In the dream, this friend and Lou were at the Los Angeles International Airport with tickets to stadium revival meetings, trying to catch a flight out, but all the terminals were closed—except United. When Lou heard this, he knew what it meant: that in these days in which God is calling us to seek revival and awakening, we will only be able to get anywhere as the body of Christ if we are united! Lou then shared that the day after this dream, United Airlines bought the naming rights to the Los Angeles Coliseum, one of the stadiums in which Lou had already held a worldwide televised prayer meeting with his ministry "The Call!" [14]

Lou also told what happened shortly after the Lord directed him to buy the Mott Auditorium, Dr. John R. Mott's old mission headquarters, in Pasadena, CA. A late 19th century, early 20th century evangelist, missionary statesman, and author of the influential book, The Evangelization of the World in this Generation,[15] first published in 1900, Dr. Mott travelled the world supporting and encouraging missionary work and preaching the Gospel. In 1946, close to the end of his life, he shared the Nobel Peace Prize for these efforts. Lou moved across the street from the old headquarters, which he re-opened as a revival prayer center.

Late one evening, Lou received a highly excitable, barely intelligible phone call from two 11-year-old Asian girls who were at that moment praying in the center with their mother and were visibly experiencing the angelic realm! When he walked over, they were pointing throughout the 3,000-seat auditorium, seeing and calling-out visions of angels and of people groups that would be reached by the gospel! Lou couldn't see any of these things, but the girls were seeing and proclaiming them! Then they began calling out: "Mott's too small! Mott's too small! We need stadiums! We need stadiums!" Suddenly, they described a vision they didn't understand: "There's Vince Lombardi in heaven!" Lou asked them, "Do you know who Vince Lombardi is?" "No," they answered, "but he has a football helmet on!" Lou told them, "He's an American football coach! He's the winning coach of the first Super Bowl!" "Lord," Lou said, "are you going to give a Super Bowl to the Church?" [16]

Lou's dream had long been to see great Gospel preaching events in stadiums throughout the United States and the world, and with his ministry The Call, he has held some of his own. By 2018, more prophetic voices in the Church began foretelling great stadium revival meetings across America beginning in the year 2020. At the June 2019 "Summer of Glory Conference," David Herzog, his wife Stephanie and Lou announced they had teamed up to host the first such meeting of 2020, "Awaken 2020," at Arizona State University's Sun Devil Stadium in Tempe, Arizona, Saturday, January 18th, 2020.[17] Shortly after this event was held and broadcast worldwide, the coronavirus hit the United States, shutting down all mass gatherings.

A RELATED REVELATION

A revelation paralleling the Mott Auditorium revelation, one given about 20 years ago by a well-known prophetic voice, the late Bob Jones, was reported by Pastor and prophet Shawn Bolz before this year's Super Bowl, Super Bowl LIV, played on 02/02/20, in Miami

Gardens, Florida.[18] (For those who would doubt the ministry of New Testament prophets, the Bible says: "And He Himself gave some to be apostles, some prophets, some evangelists, and some pastors and teachers, for the equipping of the saints for the work of the ministry, for the edifying of the body of of Christ…" Ephesians 4:11, 12).

Bob Jones prophesied, "When the Chiefs again win the Super Bowl, you will know that revival is about to come. God is raising up His apostolic chiefs." According to Shawn Bolz, since the prophecy was given, God has been raising up apostolic leaders in many spheres of influence to help bring about this revival. [19]

In a hard-fought game, despite trailing substantially at half-time, the Kansas City Chiefs won the 2020 Super Bowl, 31-20! The Chiefs have only won the Super Bowl 2 times. The last and the only other time was in 1970, 50 years ago, a length of time which for God is a "jubilee," a cause for great celebration and blessing in ancient Israel, a time in which debts were cancelled and slaves set free! This was Kansas City coach Andy Reid's 222nd victory as a coach. In its Super Bowl Commemorative Edition, the cover of *Sports Illustrated* headlined this improbable victory as a "Kingdom Comeback!"[20]

As you may be noticing, this revelation has a lot to do with the number 2, from the date the game was played, the number of Super Bowl victories by the winning team, to the number of victories the winning coach attained that day. Biblically, the number 2's main significance is unity—In marriage, as well as between Jesus

Christ and the body of Christ, and between the believer and God in prayer, which in this case may mean that as Christ's body, we need to pray-in this prophesied revival, through which many debts of sin will be cancelled and captives to sin set free!

HAS GOD'S PLAN BEEN SIDELINED?

To continue with a football analogy, has God's plan for an end-times revival and awakening been sidelined? No, of course not! God's purposes cannot be stopped. As Job answered God,

"I know that You can do all things, and that no purpose of Yours can be thwarted." (Job 42:2)

In the Bible and in daily life, God often works using numbers. Again, one of the meanings of the number 2 is unity. The Bible says, "Can two walk together, unless they be agreed?" (Amos 3:3) I believe that the Lord allowed this pandemic and its lengthening, not to stop a prophesied move of revival and awakening (or He would be working against His own purposes), but to postpone it until more of the body of Christ comes together in greater unity and strongly undergirds it with prayer!

- *Certainly, prayer has been growing during this pandemic in the body of Christ, prayers of repentance that will bring healing from it and an end to its human and economic devastation, prayers in response to national turmoil, and prayers for revival in the Church and awakening in society! This is happening in Christian homes, through prayers by phone and on social media among believers, through internet church services, and through agreement in prayer with Christian publications, radio, and T.V., in response to God's directive in 2 Chronicles 7: 14, and in response to prophecies He has given to David Wilkerson, Bob Jones and others.*

Could it be that the prophesied Third Great Awakening will begin in 2021, not in year 50, but in year 51, after the Chiefs' first victory in 1970? After all, 20 + 31, the score of this game, adds up to 51! Remember, prophet Bob Jones prophesied that when the Chiefs again won the Super Bowl, revival was *"not coming,"* but *"was about to come."* Keep the following biblical encouragement to pray in your heart and act upon it:

- **"Confess your trespasses to one another, and pray for one another, that you may be healed. The effective, fervent prayer of a righteous man avails much. Elijah was a man with a nature like ours, and he prayed earnestly that it would not rain; and it did not rain on the land for three years and six months. And he prayed again, and the earth produced its fruit." (James 5:15—18)**

At this time, we need to pray for an awakening with much spiritual fruit! For a massive harvest!

CHAPTER 5

OTHER WORDS ABOUT REVIVAL AND AWAKENING

CHAPTER OVERVIEW

There are many places through which God wants to bring revival to this nation and the world! If you have a burden for revival and awakening in your area, you don't need to wait for a "word;" God wants it; start praying-it-in with others! Get some meetings going! "A word," when we get it, is valuable as encouragement! "Word" or not, I believe our Lord wants us to partner with Him to start many revival fires in this nation, so as David Wilkerson prophesied, "a Third Great Awakening . . . will sweep across America and the world!" Prayer for revival and awakening in New Mexico and Pennsylvania is covered here as an example of what God wants to do throughout our nation and the world!

A WORD FOR SANTA FE!

In the summer of 2014, my wife Yvonne and I moved to Santa Fe, New Mexico, after having pastored a church elsewhere in New Mexico for 6 years.

We had been praying for revival and awakening in New Mexico since 2003, when we heard "words" about revival coming to New Mexico from apostle Chuck Pierce of Glory of Zion Ministries, and pastor and intercessor Dutch Sheets, at a C. Peter and Doris Wagner prayer and prophetic conference in Albuquerque. At this conference, Dutch Sheets prophesied about New Mexico: "The moving of My Spirit is on this land, and the first fruits of My Spirit will be manifested here." (See Dr. Chuck Pierce's and Pastor Dutch Sheet's book, Releasing the Prophetic Destiny of a Nation, pg. 322.) [21] In 1999, intercessor Cindy Jacobs stunningly prophesied about New Mexico: " . . . the Lord has shown me there is going to be a massive revival that comes out of this state—one that they will write about in history books. [22]

Soon after moving to Santa Fe, we heard through Pastor Judith Nowers, the leader of "Joyful Ministries," a prayer center in our city, that a man was visiting the center that had "a word about revival" for Santa Fe. Yvonne and I, along with one of our pastors, Eva Gonzales, went to the prayer center to hear him. There were about 30 people at the meeting to greet and hear Bernie Kuchta, who paid his own way from Maryland to deliver his "word." [23]

Bernie told us that he and his wife Teresa had been foreign missionaries before our Lord called them back home to the United States. Not knowing what was next for them, they began to pray. God led them to pray for America. They went to a store, bought a map of the United States and began praying over it, asking the Lord to send them wherever He wanted. The Lord immediately spoke to them about a place called "Santa Fe," revealing that there would be revival in Santa Fe. They found six "Santa Fes" on the map, so they began to ask the Lord for which "Santa Fe" they should pray and deliver the message about revival.

The very next morning, the answer came rather dramatically when Bernie went to the doctor for a check-up! While in the waiting room, he overheard the doctor twice tell one of his assistants, "I'm going to Santa Fe on vacation!" When Bernie went in to see the doctor, he immediately asked him about which "Santa Fe" he was speaking. "Santa Fe, the capital of New Mexico," was his answer, and Bernie then knew for which Santa Fe he and his wife Teresa were to pray.

They prayed for a year. After that time, Bernie sent a letter to many of the pastors in in Santa Fe, telling them that "God was going to pour out His Spirit on Santa Fe, New Mexico, and that he had a word about revival for the city." Only a few responded, but at the invitation of Pastor Nowers, Bernie came to Santa Fe to deliver his "word."

After his message, based on 2 Chronicles 7:14, which included the testimony of how he got his "word," and urging us to pray-in this "word," I asked Bernie how I could stay in touch with him. He gave me his email. My wife and I began to pray about this "word," because we knew our Lord has asked His people to pray to the Father about the harvest (see Luke 10:2) and there were biblical examples about "praying-in" prophecies, most notably by the Prophet Daniel in Daniel 9, about Israel's return to the land after the Babylonian Exile and the first disciples praying-in Jesus' prophecy about the Holy Spirit coming in power for the first time in the book of Acts (See Acts 1:8, 14 and 2:1-41). As I previously mentioned, Lou Engle has elucidated this principle well, saying, "Prophecies are an invitation to intercession." [24]

One thing that confirmed for my wife and me that we were following God's plan in praying for revival in Santa Fe, was when a friend, Mary Rodriguez, as she was moving from Santa Fe to Albuquerque, gave us a large, beautifully matted and framed photograph of a sunset landscape of Santa Fe, taken by artist Maria Randolph Hanley. Ms. Randolph called this work of art, "Santa Fe, City of Holy Faith, Jude 20-25." [25] She had long prayed, as had Mary, for revival in Santa Fe. Mary told us she wanted someone who was committed to praying for revival in Santa Fe to have this beautiful work of art, so that this city would one day live up to its great name! "Santa Fe" means "Holy Faith" in Spanish. It is located within the "Sangre de Cristo (Blood of Christ) Mountains." Would there be a better place for a revival to start? Jude verses 20-25, read:

"But you, beloved, building yourselves up on your most holy faith, praying in the Holy Spirit, keep yourselves in the love of God, looking for the mercy of our Lord Jesus Christ unto eternal life. And on some have compassion, making a distinction, but others save with fear, pulling them out of the fire, hating even the garment defiled by the flesh. Now to Him who is able to keep you from stumbling, and to present you faultless before the presence of His glory with exceeding joy, to God our Savior, who alone is wise, be glory and majesty, dominion and power, both now and forever. Amen." (Jude vs. 20—25)

UNITED PRAYER MEETINGS

In the Fall of 2019, I felt the Lord leading me to organize united prayer meetings for revival and awakening across church lines in our city. After meeting for several months, we had several Church leaders, para-Church leaders and participants meeting faithfully in prayer, one evening a month, for an hour and 15 minutes, rotating monthly between 2 churches. I was especially assisted in these efforts by my wife, Yvonne, by Pastor Judith Nowers, a faithful couple, Aaron and Rachel Dennis, Stephen Hodges, of the Santa Fe Chapter of Full Gospel Businessmen, and Jose and Micki Vasquez, who direct The Barnabas Institute, a Center for Christian community in Santa Fe, which seeks to unify the Church by providing an internet platform and mailings that communicate news about Christian ministries and events in the area, encourages prayer for the city, state, and nation, and works toward the passage of state and national laws which reflect biblical principles.

It was difficult to add members to this prayer team, as some church leaders would say to me, "We already have prayer at our church" or would not answer my phone calls. I tried to emphasize that this was a "My people" united effort, according to 2 Chronicles 7:14, something so simple yet so difficult for some leaders to grasp during a time when the Church has become so segmented. It is actually easier to invite church members, not leaders, to united prayer, and have them invite their leaders, because their leaders are more apt to trust their members than anyone else. To emphasize unity in the body of Christ, the overall plan has been to add churches to our church rotation, as people from more churches join in this prayer focus.

During this time, I got a hold of Bernie Kuchta by email to tell him what we were doing, now 5 years later. He was very excited that we were following-up on the "word" our Lord had given him and his wife Teresa for Santa Fe. He also told me he was meeting to pray with church leaders and members in Shrewsbury, PA, and that they were already seeing signs of revival there!

Just recently, Bernie and I communicated again. He emailed me that he had been leading prayer and praise revival meetings in New Freedom, PA, until the pandemic grew. They are now just starting to meet again. Bernie wrote, "There is a Christian campground within a few minutes of New Freedom called Summit Grove. I found out that evangelists would travel there in the late 1700s and 1800s to preach. In the late 1800s, people from Baltimore, Pennsylvania, Washington, D.C., Virginia, and Philadelphia would travel by train and horse and buggy to attend two weeks of revival meetings at the campgrounds. As a result, many people in the surrounding area were saved. Newspaper reports indicated that people who attended these meetings went back to their own churches and revival would break out! We are praying that the clogged wells of revival at Summit Grove would again open and flood, not only that area, but the entire U.S. and the world!"

- ***To this point, there are many places through which God wants to bring revival to this nation and the world! If you have a burden for revival and awakening in your*** *area, you don't need to wait for a "word;" God wants it; start praying-it-in with others! Get some meetings going! "A word," when we get it, is valuable as encouragement! If you want to be encouraged by knowing what recent "words" have been given for your state in God's plan for revival and awakening, start with the book, <u>Releasing the Prophetic Destiny of a Nation</u>.* [26] *"Word" or not, I believe our Lord wants us to partner with Him to start many revival fires in this nation, so as David Wilkerson prophesied, "a Third Great Awakening . . . will sweep across America and the world!"* [27]

- Pray as the Prophet Jeremiah did as he sought the Lord's blessing on Israel:

"'Ah, Lord God! Behold, You have made the heavens and the earth by Your great power and outstretched arm. There is nothing too hard for You." (Jeremiah 32:17)

- Do as the Lord told the Prophet Jeremiah to do:

"Call to Me, and I will answer you, and show you great and mighty things, which you do not know." (Jeremiah 33:3)

- *A United Prayer Pattern in Santa Fe*

In our United Prayer Meetings in Santa Fe, we follow a simple pattern, reproduced in this book's appendix, to maximize participation by churches of different traditions and among those attending. Briefly, we have an introduction explaining prayer for revival and awakening, a short praise and worship time, spontaneous prayer in groups of 3 or 4 for a time (so everyone has a chance to pray), spontaneous prayer as a whole body for a time, and a closing prayer. To promote unity by trying to avoid differences over the style and length of the service, we focus the service mainly on praying for revival and awakening (although some understandably, pray for the salvation of family and friends, healing, an end to the pandemic and to other corporate disasters, etc., something we don't want to limit), providing Bible verses and prayer foci in our service guide for people to use in praying, keeping the length of the meeting to 1 hr. 15 min., and only operating in the gifts of the Spirit during the meeting when permitted to do so by a host church, or in an "afterglow," if given the freedom by the host church to have this extended time. Again, the appendix of this book consists of an example of this suggested prayer pattern.

My wife and I are again starting our monthly United Prayer Meetings in Santa Fe by telephone conference call or Zoom, until we can again meet together in person. United Prayer in Santa Fe is just one of several prayer movements for revival and awakening that have recently started in New Mexico, most notably, one ignited across New Mexico by revivalist and pastor Caleb Cooper, Pastor of New Hope Revival Church, Truth or Consequences, NM (What a consequential place name for a revival movement to be birthed!), and author of 2 notable books on revival and awakening, <u>Pioneering Prophetic Patterns of Purpose: When Encountering God Leads to Another Encounter</u>,[28] and <u>Jesus</u>

Focused: Awakening Endtime Prophetic Strategy.[29] There is also an active prayer movement for revival led by a group of pastors in Española, NM, among them Pastor J.D. Miera of Victory Faith Foursquare Church and Pastor Barry Trujillo of New Creation in Christ Ministries. There may be other prayer movements that have started across New Mexico as well, about whom I am not aware.

ONE DREAM

At times, God speaks to me through dreams. He gave me two key dreams while we were starting our united prayer effort in Santa Fe. I believe both could be important revelations for the success of any united prayer effort in the body of Christ, especially in America.

In the first dream, which I call "The Para-Church Ministry Dream," I was travelling in a pick-up truck up a paved road on a very steep hill. Suddenly, there was a huge, heavy, high, 2-sided closed steel door blocking the entire roadway! I got out of the truck to check it out and found it was locked and could only be opened by a key. While I was wondering what to do next, I was joined by a group of men, one of which provided the key I used to unlock the door and get through. The very evening before I had this dream, our united prayer group had met and I had asked Jose Vasquez, who with his wife heads the Barnabas Center for Christian Community in Santa Fe, if the Full Gospel Businessmen of which I knew he was a part were still meeting. He said "yes," and invited me to the next meeting the following week. I was planning to present the vision of United Prayer for Revival and Awakening in Santa Fe to this group.

After having this dream, I realized the Lord was telling me that the Full Gospel Businessmen would be key to the success of our united prayer effort in Santa Fe, because as a para-Church organization, its members attended many churches in our city and they could invite the leaders and members of their churches to participate. At the actual meeting, my message on united prayer received a good reception and I do believe this group will be a key to the success of our efforts going forward! We will get through the "huge, heavy, high steel door" that often stands as a barrier to united work among churches in many communities! I also felt that as the road in my dream was going upwards on a hill, this effort will take this para-Church group and the churches in our city to greater heights of prayer and ministry! So let your contacts with para-Church ministries help propel united prayer for revival and awakening in your area!

As a point of interest, on the way to my first meeting with the Full Gospel Businessmen, I ran into an actual road- block, not on a hill, but a roadblock nonetheless, in which an electrical line was sprawled over the roadway, due to a storm the night before! For safety's sake, a police car was blocking the passage of traffic. This spoke to me that regardless of how my message would be received at the meeting that morning, as there may be "static" from some who don't believe in the power of prayer for revival and awakening or would want to "short-circuit" any message by a newcomer, we must find a way, as I did that morning by taking a detour, to meet with para-Church people, as many are good-hearted, and willing to assist with efforts toward revival and awakening! And so it was!

A SECOND DREAM

A second dream, which I call "The Frozen Tradition Dream," was troubling. I found myself in a church, in the pastor's office, waiting to meet with him about united prayer. He was late for our meeting, so I walked outside the office and noticed a long line of people lined up to get votive candles, which I figured were for a funeral. At that point, the pastor arrived. When I asked him what the people were doing, he said they were lining up to attend a baptism. In my mind, I questioned this, but said nothing. Then we walked into his office. As he closed the door to meet with me, I noticed that the inside of the door was decorated with intricate patterns on gray-colored wood, and the dream was over.

What struck me about this dream and gave me its message was that, first of all, the pastor was late. He arrived in a hurry and seemed to want to get the meeting over quickly, because he was attending to matters that to him were more important—more important than united prayer. When he arrived, he described those who were lined-up as entering a baptism, while I felt they were entering a funeral. In other words, he stated that they were entering for "life" and I felt they were entering for "death." I interpret this as churches who are less focused on the life God offers and more focused on the church's dead traditions or habitual ways of doing things. Finally, the intricate patterns in gray inside of the pastor's office door speak of ingrained traditions, to which a pastor or church are committed, like commitment to a denomination or association as a first priority, various theologies, certain biblical interpretations, the church's own programs and prayer meetings that cannot be altered, or even the pastors' or church members' secret sins (remember, these patterns were inside the office door, usually out of sight), all of which do not easily allow for cooperation in life-giving prayer with others in the body of Christ! Gray is also the color of compromise, as these traditions, theologies, and activities may compromise or sins will compromise our walk with God and our unity with others in Christ. We need to pray that all pastors, church members, and churches in our communities who have such ingrained attitudes and issues will repent so that they can join the rest of the body of Christ in seeking the revived and joyful life God offers and praying for the world's awakening to Jesus!

CHAPTER 6

"FROM THAT TO THIS"

CHAPTER OVERVIEW

In the midst of our fledging united prayer effort, the COVID-19 pandemic hit our state. We went from prayer for a prophesied city-wide revival, a prophesied state revival, and anticipation of nationwide stadium revivals, to prayer at home as individuals, as couples, as families, or by phone or internet groups, but this does not limit God!

HEARING FROM THE LORD

As Mary did in her home in "Mary and Martha's Story" in the Bible (see Luke 10:38-42), we need to make time to spend with the Lord and hear from Him. For us, it would be hearing from Him through the Scriptures and through the Holy Spirit, especially in prayer. The Lord looks forward to revealing truth about Himself, about us, and about life, when we spend time with Him. As Jesus said about Mary:

"But one thing is needed, and Mary has chosen that good part, which will not be taken away from her." (Luke 10:42)

During this pandemic, God has been teaching us more about hearing the Lord and the power of prayer to our God.

When my wife and I pray together, we usually play worship music at a low volume on one of our phones to have a peaceful background. You do not have to do so, but as Pentecostal Christians, we interject our praying with our prayer language (tongues), which helps our prayer flow more easily, and provides meditation time for each of us to receive more revelation as to what to pray.

We do not bring a prayer list to our prayer time, but sometimes at the beginning of our prayer time, we briefly mention some problems of importance, and people or issues we want to make sure we cover in our prayer that evening. Praying night after night helps us more easily remember the many people and topics we are praying about. Our prayer times are focused on praying for revival in the Church and awakening to God in society, as well as the current pandemic, other corporate disasters, and other issues facing our nation, but also includes praying for salvation and problems in our families and for others we know.

- *At times, God brings to mind a verse, or a whole chapter or Psalm in the Bible to read during our prayer time, and pray through. Sometimes we repeat promises of God in Scripture and pray about them. Sometimes, we just worship the Lord and pray for periods of time in tongues.*

- *Sometimes, during our prayer times, we pray The Lord's Prayer in detail, expanding on each phrase in this prayer (see, for example, The Lord's Prayer in Matthew 6:9-13), or pray other prayers found in Scripture, such as those prayed by the Apostle Paul (see, for example, Paul's prayers in his letter to the Ephesians: Ephesians 1:15-2:7, and Ephesians 3:14-21), Daniel's prayers in the Old Testament, or other prayers prayed by people in the Bible, such as David in the Psalms, that we can pray along with. Praying these can help focus our prayer time, and are often just what we need to pray, or just what others need us to pray for them in various life situations.*

Now that my wife and I are praying more, we are anticipating more breakthroughs in our lives, our family, the church, the body of Christ, our city, our state, our nation and our world! Life, in fact, has become very exciting! We are experiencing the following words of our Lord in a more vivid way:

"Again I say to you that if two of you agree on earth concerning anything that they ask, it will be done for them by my Father in heaven. For where two or three are gathered together in My name, I am there in the midst of them." (Matthew 18:19, 20)

PRAYING WITH AUTHORITY

As should all Christians, we are also praying with authority! Remember, God the Father has:

". . . raised us up together, and made us sit together in the heavenly places in Christ Jesus." (Ephesians 2:6)

As His redeemed sons and daughters, the Father has allowed us to spiritually sit on thrones (seats of authority) beside Jesus, sharing in His Son's spiritual authority, when we are repentant, and aligned with the truth of His Word, in life and prayer.

In Jesus' "Parable of the Prodigal Son" in Luke 15, the Father, in v. 22, gives us the Robe of Righteousness (because of the blood of Jesus that cleanses us from sin), the signet ring of authority (to act as "power of attorney" in His behalf), and the sandals of a son or daughter (only slaves went barefoot in those days, not sons and daughters, which signify that we are free to pray and act on God's behalf, when we do so in accordance with His Word.).

Jesus tells us:

"Behold, I give you the authority to trample on serpents and scorpions, and over all the power of the enemy, and nothing shall by any means hurt you." (Luke 10:19)

"Assuredly, I say to you, whatever you bind on earth will be bound in heaven, and whatever you loose on earth will be loosed in heaven." (Matthew 18:18)

The Word of God tells us:

"Let us therefore come boldly to the throne of grace, that we may obtain mercy and find grace to help in time of need." (Hebrews 4:16)

A DREAM ABOUT PRAYING WITH AUTHORITY

When my wife and I were pastoring our last church, I had what was for us a significant dream, which could also be a helpful revelation for you. In it, I found myself in a dark room with three large, brown, leather armchairs on a raised platform. I immediately felt they were thrones—that one of them was the Lord's and two of them belonged to my wife and me. The Lord's throne was clean and being used, but ours were very dusty and unused. In the dream, I realized that I needed to get onto my throne. As I walked toward my throne, a mean, snarling, dark-colored dog suddenly appeared to try to keep me from doing so! I was scared, but found the courage to kick it out of the way, and got up on my throne (I am not advocating the kicking of dogs here. This dog, in the dream, I believe stood for Satan.).

Because our thrones were dusty, this dream revealed to me that my wife and I were not sitting and praying from our thrones, that is, we were not praying from a place of authority. Often, we were praying pleading prayers when we needed to be praying prayers of authority—binding Satan and his demons, breaking their power, loosing the power of God, and declaring and decreeing God's Word, will and kingdom to come into different situations of our lives and other people's lives, in Jesus' name! Now, God will listen when we "cry out" to Him, but when we know what His will is (when it lines up with both His written Word and what His Spirit is telling us), we need to pray with authority, declaring and decreeing that God's specific will be done in any given situation.

The angry dog, who stood for Satan, will try to keep us from taking our rightful place, seated beside Christ on our thrones, praying with Christ's authority (in His all-powerful name), because that makes us dangerous to him and to his kingdom of darkness. We cannot neglect our authority in Christ or succumb to Satan's efforts to accuse us or shame us if have repented of sin or listen to his lies about our inadequacies, that say we do not belong on those thrones. Through Christ, the Father forgives, restores and makes us adequate to serve Him! Instead, we need to kick Satan out of the way, take our rightful places alongside Christ and begin praying with authority that God's kingdom will come on earth as it is in heaven!

After this revelation, our faith increased, our prayers became more powerful, and we saw God move in amazing ways in our lives, in the lives of people for whom we prayed, in our ministry, in the community, and in other situations about which we prayed!

The book of Job says the following about praying from a point of repentance, communion with God, and authority:

"Now acquaint yourself with Him, and be at peace; thereby good will come to you. Receive, please, instruction from his mouth, and lay up his words in your heart. If you return to the Almighty, you will be built up; you will remove iniquity far from your tents. Then you will lay your gold in the dust, and the gold of Ophir among the stones of the brooks. Yes, the Almighty will be your gold and your precious silver; for then you will have your delight in the Almighty, and lift your

face to God. You will make your prayer to Him, He will hear you, and you will pay your vows. You will also declare a thing, and it will be established for you; so light will shine on your ways. When they cast you down, and you say, 'Exaltation will come!,' then He will save the humble person. He will even deliver one who is not innocent; Yes, he will be delivered by the purity of your hands." (Job 22:21—30)

UNITED TO GIVE A WITNESS

As the Body of Christ we need to be more united, not just to pray in the face of disaster, but to give a witness to the world about the reality, love and power of Jesus Christ! As Lou Engle says, "Only a united Church can heal a divided nation!" [30] Our Lord says in John Chapter 17, that when the world sees us loving each other, it will believe that we have Someone who has truly come from heaven, loves us, has shown us how to love each other, and loves them!

"I do not pray for these alone, but also for those who will believe in Me through their word; that they all may be one, as You, Father, are in Me, and I in You; that they also may be one in Us, that the world may believe that You sent Me. And the glory which You gave Me I have given them, that they may be one just as We are one; I in them, and You in Me; that they may be one just as We are one: I in them, and You in Me; that they may be made perfect in one, and that the world may know that You have sent Me, and have loved them as You have loved Me." (John 17:20—24)

Pastor Daniel Castillo, M.Div.

PRAYING AS THE BODY OF CHRIST FOR REPENTANCE AND GRACE

We need to remember what our Lord said to Christians in Laodicea in Asia Minor long ago, which still applies to us today: that He does not want us to be lukewarm—to compromise with sin—and that He "stands at the door of our hearts and knocks," more than willing to come in and fellowship with us when we repent. He is also willing to restore us to our place of authority as His sons and daughters, including our authority in prayer, when we repent:

"I know your works, that you are neither cold or hot. I could wish you were cold or hot. So then, because you are lukewarm, and neither cold nor hot, I will vomit you out of My mouth. Because you say, 'I am rich, have become wealthy, and have need of nothing'—and do not know that you are wretched, miserable, poor, blind and naked—I counsel you to buy from Me gold refined in the fire, that you may be rich; and white garments, that you may be clothed, that the shame of your nakedness may not be revealed; and anoint your eyes with eye salve, that you may see. As many as I love, I rebuke and chasten. Therefore be zealous and repent. Behold I stand at the door and knock. If anyone hears My voice and opens the door, I will come in to him and dine with Him, and he with Me. To him who overcomes I will grant to sit with Me on My throne, as I also overcame and sat down with My Father on His throne." (Revelation 3:15—21)

The apostle Peter says that if Christians humble themselves and repent, they will receive God's grace, that is, His undeserved favor. Isn't God's undeserved favor what we most need right now?

50

"God resists the proud, but gives grace to the humble. Therefore humble yourselves under the mighty hand of God, that He may exalt you in due time, casting all your care upon Him, for He cares for you." (1 Peter 5:5—7)

PRAYING FOR A WORLD WHOM GOD LOVES

"For God so loved the world that He gave His only begotten Son, that whoever believes in Him should not perish, but have everlasting life." (John 3:16)

We need to pray for the world with a heart of love. Many are lost and don't know God. For many, pleasure has become a god. Sports is a religion to many. For many, sex is only using others, sometimes many others, for selfish pleasure, not a gift that God intends we enjoy in a committed, loving, marriage relationship. Business success, material things, food, travel, entertainment, games, and many other activities, while not bad in themselves, can be escapes from reality that keep people from making their lives right with God and others. Escapes into addictions can be deadly. People ignore God to run after sin. Others have distorted ideas about God, taught by erroneous religious systems or by godless philosophies. We need to pray that people will understand they are loved by the true God and His Son, Jesus Christ, a God who is ready to forgive, give them eternal life, show them how to live fulfilled, transformed lives and to avoid many consequences of sin on earth, and eternal hell:

"And this is eternal life, that they may know You, the only true God, and Jesus Christ whom You have sent." (John 17:3)

WE CAN PRAY WITH EMPATHY

Along with other people, Christians have suffered in this pandemic. Because we too, have suffered, we can more easily identify with broken people who come into our lives, helping them receive the love and comfort we've received from God.

"Blessed be the God and Father of our Lord Jesus Christ, the Father of mercies and God of all comfort, who comforts us in all our tribulation, that we may be able to comfort those who are in any trouble, with the comfort with which we ourselves are comforted by God. For as the sufferings of Christ abound in us, so our consolation also abounds through Christ. Now if we are afflicted, it is for your consolation and salvation, which is effective for enduring the same sufferings which we also suffer. Or if we are comforted, it is for your consolation and salvation." (2 Corinthians 1:3—6)

THERE HAVE BEEN MANY HEALINGS!

There have been many healings from this pandemic, through the compassionate efforts of medical professionals, who have put their lives on the line for others, to whom God has given strength and insight, and researchers to whom God has given wisdom and understanding to develop anti-viral medicines and other therapeutic treatments, by God-given antibodies in our bodies destroying the virus although we aren't aware of it, but also by the miraculous power of God! Through Christian media, we have heard of amazing healings from COVD-19, in answer to prayer!

FORGIVENESS AND HEALING THROUGH COMMUNION

- *Every evening, after each of our prayer times, my wife Yvonne and I take communion, which symbolizes what God has done through his Son Jesus Christ to offer us forgiveness and eternal life. We also pray for others who need forgiveness and salvation. But taken in faith, the grape juice of communion not only symbolizes the blood of Christ shed to pay the penalty for our sins, so we could be forgiven and have a relationship with God, it is also about the blood of Christ that can physically heal:*

  "But He was wounded for our transgressions, He was bruised for our iniquities; The chastisement for our peace was upon Him, and by His stripes we are healed." (Isaiah 53:5)

- *So we also pray for our healing from any ailments when we take communion, and the healing of others, through the blood of Christ.*

As evangelist Perry Stone has well-written, spiritually and physically, communion is The Meal that Heals. [31]

Psalm 91

- *Often, we also pray Psalm 91 over ourselves and our family. That our Lord answers the affirmations of Psalm 91 is abundantly clear through the testimonies of many Christians! A book that has gathered many such testimonies of God's powerful deliverance by trusting His promises in Psalm 91, is Peggy Joyce Ruth's and Angelia Ruth Schum's <u>Psalm 91</u>,[32] which I highly recommend to anyone who may doubt this. Following are three of many verses from Psalm 91 we can pray over ourselves and our loved ones during this time of COVID-19 and other disasters:*

"Surely He shall deliver you from the snare of the fowler and from the perilous pestilence. He shall cover you with His feathers, and under His wings you shall take refuge; . . ." (Psalm 91:3—4b)

"You shall not be afraid of the terror by night, not of the arrow that flies by day, nor of the pestilence that walks in darkness, nor of the destruction that lays waste at noonday. A thousand may fall at your side, and ten thousand at your right hand; but it shall not come near you." (Psalm 91:5—7)

"Because you have made the Lord, who is my refuge, even the Most High, your dwelling place, no evil shall befall you, not shall any plague come near your dwelling; for He shall give His angels charge over you, to keep you in all your ways." (Psalm 91:9—11)

BINDING AND CASTING OUT FEAR

In this situation of pandemic and other disasters, in the name of Jesus, we must also bind and cast out spirits of fear which may be oppressing us and others, for fear paralyzes us, keeps us from trusting God, from living in faith that He can protect us, and believing that He is in control of all is happening and has purposes in it. Fear also keeps us from experiencing miracles.

"For God has not given us a spirit of fear, but of power and of love and of a sound mind." (2 Timothy 1:7)

"Be anxious for nothing, but in everything by prayer and supplication, with thanksgiving, let your requests be made known to God; and the peace of God, which surpasses all understanding, will guard your hearts and minds through Christ Jesus." (Philippians 4:19, 20)

". . . casting all your care upon Him, for He cares for you." (I Peter 5:7)

Jesus said to Jairus, the ruler of the synagogue, whose daughter had died, before He raised her from the dead:

"Do not be afraid, only believe." (Mark 5:36c)

Because Jairus and his wife believed, they experienced a life-changing miracle!

CHAPTER 7

PRAYER THAT WILL AWAKEN AMERICA AND THE WORLD!

CHAPTER OVERVIEW

The prophet Joel says that with repentant, united prayer may come "a blessing" God may "leave behind Him!" Our prayer for our nation and world must be for: ". . . repentance toward God and faith toward our Lord Jesus Christ" (Acts 20:21), and this blessing!

GOD MAY LEAVE A BLESSING!

"Now, therefore," says the Lord, "Turn to Me with all your heart, with fasting, with weeping, and with mourning." So rend your heart, and not your garments; Return to the Lord your God, for He is gracious and merciful, slow to anger and of great kindness: And He relents from doing harm. Who knows if He will turn and relent, and leave a blessing behind Him . . . ?" (Joel 2:12—14a)

The blessing God may "leave behind Him" after repentant, united prayer, is revival and its many benefits among God's people: a people's willingness to obey God, changed lives, personal integrity, sound decision-making, lack of personal vices, little crime, much less injustice, the diminishing of poverty, loving and intact families, family prosperity, business success, the strengthening of churches, unity in governance, the exaltation of a land or nation, and the furtherance of the Gospel. Many such blessings resulted from the revivals and awakenings throughout history. One well-documented example are the blessings resulting from the Welsh Revival of 1904-1905.[33] At this time in history, blessings God will "leave behind" include the healing of our nation and world from a disastrous pandemic, healing from other nationwide and worldwide disasters, and a much-awaited last-days nationwide and worldwide awakening to God!

PRAYER THAT WILL BLESS AMERICA AND THE WORLD!

- *We must pray for our nation, that it will continue to be a city on a hill, that the nations of world will continue to see a nation based on the principles of the Word of God, that its people will continue to take the light of the Gospel throughout the world, that its government will continue to be founded on the biblical principles underlying our founding documents, that we will elect leaders who will protect religious freedom and uphold the rule of law, that God will deliver us from godless leaders and godless political systems, and that God will heal our land, both physically and spiritually! Our prayer for our nation and world must be for:*

". . . repentance toward God, and faith toward our Lord Jesus Christ (Acts 20:21)," and the blessings of revival and awakening!

- *For the world, these may very well be the last days of history as we know it—the end of the Age of Grace. Israel is God's alarm clock! It is back in its Promised Land after 2000 years! For a long generation, God has performed many miracles to establish it in a hostile environment! Prophetic voices are telling us that even more fearful things than the current pandemic are coming upon the earth! If ever we need awakening in America and the world, it is now! God wants transformed hearts, so He can shed his healing grace on America and the world, gather a massive harvest of souls, and have many people populate heaven, not hell. We must pray for revival in the Church and awakening for America and the world! It will be prayer that will awaken America and the world!*

PRAYER TO A HOLY, YET LOVING GOD

The Prophet Habakkuk said:

"O Lord, I have heard Your speech and was afraid; . . . " (Habakkuk 3:2a)

Why was the Prophet Habakkuk afraid when he heard God? Because He heard His words of judgment concerning sin. He was afraid because God is a holy God that has to judge sin. But the Prophet concludes with a prayer:

"O Lord, revive Your work in the midst of the years! In the midst of the years make it known; In wrath remember mercy." (Habakkuk 2:2b, c, d)

- *God hates sin but loves the sinner. He hates sin because of what it does to the sinner and to other people and because unrepentant sin separates the sinner from Him, now, and if not repented of, forever! Despite God's holy wrath toward sin, let's pray with Habakkuk that "in the midst of the years" (at this very time), our Lord, who loves sinners, will, instead of requiring just judgment, remember mercy and revive His work of salvation!*

CHAPTER 8

AN UNEXPECTED DISCOVERY! DELIVERANCE AND BLESSING!

CHAPTER OVERVIEW

2 Chronicles Chapter 20:1—30 is an example, or case study, of what happens when God's people are faced with disaster and follow God's instructions in 2 Chronicles 7:12—14! God wants to deliver us and Bless Us!

PRAY IN UNITY, HUMILITY AND REPENTANCE!

Writing the final chapter of this handbook was totally unexpected! It came about during an evening of prayer with my wife Yvonne. At one point in our prayer time, the Lord directed me to read 2 Chronicles 20:1—30, about Israel facing an enemy attack when Jehoshaphat was king of Judah. 2 Chronicles 2:20 begins:

"It happened after this that the people of Moab with the people of Ammon, and others with them besides the Ammonites,

came to battle against Jehoshaphat. Then some came and told Jehoshaphat, saying, 'A great multitude is coming against you from beyond the sea, from Syria, and they are in Hazazon Tamar' (which is En Gedi). And Jehoshaphat feared, and set himself to seek the Lord, and proclaimed a fast throughout all Judah. So Judah gathered together to ask help from the Lord; and from all the cities of Judah they came to seek the Lord." (2 Chronicles 20:1—4)

King Jehoshaphat and God's people did what they should have done when facing disaster: they fasted, and humbled themselves by gathering together before the temple in united prayer, asking God for help! 2 Chronicles 2:20 continues:

"Then Jehoshaphat stood in the assembly of Judah and Jerusalem, in the house of the Lord, before the new court, and said: 'O Lord God of our fathers, are You not God in heaven and do You not rule over all the kingdoms of the nations, and in Your hand is there not power and might, so that no one is able to withstand You? Are you not our God, who drove out the inhabitants of this land before Your people Israel, and gave it to the descendants of Abraham Your friend forever? And they dwell in it, and have built You a sanctuary in it for Your name, saying: 'If disaster comes upon us—sword, judgment, pestilence, or famine—we will stand before this temple and in Your presence (for Your name is in this temple), and cry out to You in our affliction, and You will hear and save.' " (2 Chronicles 20:5—9)

In this prayer, we see that King Jehoshaphat was familiar with Scripture, knowing of the greatness of God, His sovereignty over the nations, His mighty works of love and care for His people in the past, and His power and might! This knowledge strengthened his faith as he led God's people in prayer in front of the temple.

AN UNEXPECTED DISCOVERY!

As I continued reading Jehoshaphat's prayer, I unexpectedly discovered something I had never noticed though I've read this Scripture many times before! In 2 Chronicles 20: 5--9, Jehoshaphat directly refers to God's previous words to Israel in 2 Chronicles 7:13, 14! In 2 Chronicles 20:5--9, when Jehoshaphat and the people ask God to "hear and to save," they are standing on God's promises in 2 Chronicles 7: 12—14 to "hear" and deliver! Here is 2 Chronicles 7:12—14:

"Then the Lord appeared to Solomon by night, and said to him: 'I have heard your prayer, and have chosen this place for Myself as a house of sacrifice. When I shut up heaven and there is no rain or command the locusts to devour the land, or send pestilence among My people, 'If My people, who are called by My name will humble themselves, and pray and seek My face, and turn from their wicked ways, then I will hear from heaven, and will forgive their sin and heal their land.' "
(2 Chronicles 7:12—14)

Jehoshaphat led the people in this prayer about 100 years <u>after</u> God first spoke the words in 2 Chronicles 7:12—14! (Solomon reigned between 970-931 B.C. Jehoshaphat reigned between 873-849 B.C.) Do you see the similarity between both Bible passages?

This means that this entire account in 2 Chronicles 20:1—30 is an example, or case study, of what happens when God's people are faced with disaster and follow God's instructions in 2 Chronicles 7:13, 14! As Jehoshaphat followed God's instructions in 2 Chronicles 7:13 and 14 and stood on its promises, so can we today!

WOULD GOD JUDGE HIS PEOPLE AND THE WORLD WITH CORPORATE DISASTER?

In 2 Chronicles 20:5—9, Jehoshaphat and the people of Judah had certainly humbled themselves, gathering together before the temple and praying as a united people in the face of "disaster," which Jehoshaphat describes as either "sword, judgment, pestilence, or famine." They had repented, as evidenced by their fasting and Jehoshaphat's reference to "judgment" (Note that here, God's "judgment" is part of the entire concept of God allowing "disaster," as is clearly implied in 2 Chronicles 7:13 and 14.). They were experiencing "sword" at this time, but notice Jehoshaphat's reference in verse 9 to "pestilence" as one of the disasters that can also come upon God's people.

Some say that a loving God does not "send" pestilence, so something must be wrong with the translation of the Bible in 2 Chronicles 7:13, 14. They either say that 1) God is only good and would not send such a thing, especially upon His people, and that He loves the world too much to do that to people, while others say that 2) since there is no pestilence in heaven, He would not send pestilence on earth, that is, that He only does on earth what He does in heaven. Pestilence, and any other disaster, they say, can only come from Satan, or just from the fact that we live in a world broken through sin.

The Bible, however, clearly states in 2 Chronicles 7:13, 14, that the Lord can send disaster as judgment for sin (see v. 13). Throughout the Bible, God uses Satan, the actual agent of disaster, to bring it, and then is able to use it against him, to accomplish His purposes. Remember, in the book of Job, God allowed Satan to afflict Job (Job 1 and 2), then used Job's experience with affliction to instruct and strengthen Job spiritually, restore him and instruct His people through Job's experience (the rest of the book of Job).

In 1 Corinthians 5:4, 5, the apostle Paul, "in the name of our Lord Jesus Christ," "delivered" a disobedient Christian "to Satan for the destruction of the flesh, that his spirit may be saved in the day of the Lord Jesus." Basing themselves on these verses, Christians can rightly say, "God takes the body to spare the soul," that is, God may strike a Christian who is practicing sin with sickness, tragedy or other difficulties, so that this may cause him to repent, so instead of going to hell, he may go to heaven. Why then, can't God strike the Church and the world with pestilence or other disasters for the same purpose? Admittedly, many Christians are not living lives of sin, but we are part of a world that suffers because of sin.

BELIEVE IN THE LORD . . . BELIEVE HIS PROPHETS!

Back to 2 Chronicles Chapter 20. How did Israel's case study turn out? Let's see. Jehoshaphat continues his prayer:

". . . For we have no power against this great multitude that is coming against us; nor do we know what to do, but our eyes are upon You." (2 Chronicles 20:12b, c)

Here is a people's total dependence upon God! The narrative continues:

"Now all Judah, with their little ones, their wives, and their children, stood before the Lord. Then the Spirit of the Lord came upon Jahaziel the son of Zechariah, the son of Mattaniah, a Levite of the sons of Asaph, in the midst of the assembly. And he said, 'Listen, all you of Judah and you inhabitants of Jerusalem, and you, King Jehoshaphat!' Thus says the Lord to you: 'Do not be afraid because of this great multitude, for the battle is not yours, but God's. Tomorrow go down against them. . . . You will not need to fight in this battle. Position yourselves, stand still and see the salvation of the Lord, who is with you, O Judah and Jerusalem! Do not fear or be dismayed: tomorrow go out against them, for the Lord is with you.'" (2 Chronicles 20:14-17)

Here, God's prophetic word comes by the Spirit of the Lord to Jahaziel, a Levite, a man of the sons of Asaph (The sons of Asaph were a group of temple worship leaders.). Prophets tend to be worshipers, because in their attitude of worship, they are attuned to hear God.

This was Jehoshaphat's and the people of Judah's response to God's prophetic word:

"And Jehoshaphat bowed his head with his face to the ground, and all Judah and the inhabitants of Jerusalem bowed before the Lord, worshiping the Lord. Then the Levites of the children of the Kohathites and of the children of the Korahites stood up to praise the Lord God of Israel with voices loud and high. So they rose early in the morning and went out into the Wilderness of Tekoa: and as they went out, Jehoshaphat stood and said, 'Hear me, O Judah and you inhabitants of Jerusalem: Believe in the Lord your God, and you shall be established; believe His prophets, and you shall prosper.'" (2 Chronicles 20:18—20)

Here Jehoshaphat tells the people of Judah something that the Church today should hear: "Believe in the Lord your God . . . believe His prophets!" In the midst of this pandemic or any disaster, we all need to "believe His prophets," biblical and modern-day, who say that we can trust God to fight our battles and deliver us, when we stand in faith!

BY FAITH, SING, PRAISE AND DRIVE OUT FEAR; IN FAITH STAND STILL AND SEE GOD GIVE THE VICTORY!

"And when he had consulted with the people, he appointed those who should praise the Lord, and who should praise the beauty of holiness, as they went out before the army and were saying: 'Praise the Lord, for His mercy endures forever.' Now when they began to sing and to praise, the Lord set ambushes against the people of Ammon, Moab, and Mount Seir, who had come against Judah; and they were defeated. For the people of Ammon and Moab stood up against the inhabitants of Mount Seir to utterly kill and destroy them. And when they had made an end of the inhabitants of Seir, they helped to destroy one another. So when Judah came to a place overlooking the wilderness, they looked toward the multitude; and there were their dead bodies, fallen on the earth. No one had escaped." (2 Chronicles 20:22—24)

Three things stand out in this account: 1) After consulting the people, the King appointed some to praise the Lord and the "beauty of holiness" (The "beauty of holiness," speaks of the Lord's character that cannot tolerate sin. These enemies were sinfully attacking Judah, doing so for purely personal gain and to dominate them, although the people of Israel had never attacked them in the past.). 2) Why did the king consult the people? Because he was looking for volunteers who had the faith to go out before the army with nothing but praise, saying: "Praise the Lord, for His mercy endures forever!" 3) It was "when they began to sing and to praise," that "the Lord set ambushes" against Judah's enemies and "they were defeated!"

Sending volunteer "praisers" before the army was not an afterthought. This was done so the faith of the "praisers" would give the army faith and drive fear from their hearts! As the prophet Jahaziel prophesied, they were not to be afraid, for they did not need to fight in this battle! The battle was not theirs, but God's! Israel's army just had to "position themselves" in faith, and God would work, because He works when people trust Him! They were to "stand still," trust in Him, "and see the salvation of the Lord!" God then caused Judah's enemies to fight each other! This is why the Bible says:

"But without faith it is impossible to please Him, for he who comes to God must believe that He is, and that He is a rewarder of those who diligently seek Him." (Hebrews 11:6)

- **The most often repeated commandment in the Bible is "Fear not!" When we unite, as the Body of Christ, in repentant prayer, and trust God to act, God will answer our prayers when we face personal battles and corporate disasters, and bring revival and awakening!**

BY FAITH, PUT ON THE WHOLE ARMOR OF GOD AND DRIVE OUT FEAR; STAND IN FAITH AND SEE GOD GIVE US THE VICTORY!

Ephesians 6:10-18, is the New Testament's parallel passage to 2 Chronicles 20:1-30. In it, the apostle Paul tells us how we can face any circumstance with confidence in God and see Him give us the victory! To do so, Paul tells us to "put on the whole armor of God."

"Finally, my brethren, be strong in the Lord and in the power of His might. Put on the whole armor of God, that you may be able to stand against the wiles of the devil. For we do not wrestle against flesh and blood, but against principalities, against powers, against the rulers of the darkness of this age, against spiritual hosts of wickedness in the heavenly places. Therefore take up the whole armor of God, that you may be able to withstand in the evil day, and having done all, to stand. Stand therefore, having girded your waist with truth, having put on the breastplate of righteousness, and having shod your feet with the preparation of the gospel of peace; above all, taking the shield of faith with which, you will be able to quench all the fiery darts of the wicked one. And take the helmet of salvation, and the sword of the Spirit, which is the word of God; praying always with all prayer and supplication in the Spirit, being watchful to this end with all perseverance and supplication for all the saints—and for me, that I may open my mouth boldly to make known the mystery of the gospel . . . "(Ephesians 6:10—19)

As we "put on this armor" in prayer, we "put on confidence," or "faith in God!" We become "strong in the Lord and in the power of His might!" Then, we are able to "withstand in the evil day," and "having done all, to stand" in faith and see God give us the victory!

- **If we, the Body of Christ, pray in unity and repentance, "put on the whole armor of God" in the face of this pandemic and any other disaster, "are strong in the Lord and in the power of His might," and "stand" in faith, God will give us and our nation the victory, and "a Third Great Awakening . . . will sweep America and the world!"** [34]

There are seven parts to our spiritual armor, most of it fashioned after the armor of the Roman soldier of the apostle Paul's day: 1) the belt of truth, 2) the breastplate of righteousness, 3) the sandals of the gospel of peace, 4) the shield of faith, 5) the helmet of salvation, 6) the sword of the Spirit, which is the word of God, and 7) prayer! About the armor: 1) "The belt of truth" is all biblical truth, 2) "the breastplate of righteousness" is the righteousness God applies to us through the forgiveness we receive through Christ and the righteousness that God is working in us by the Holy Spirit and His Word, 3) "the sandals of the gospel of peace" symbolize our standing as His adopted sons and daughters, brothers and sisters of His Son, 4) "the shield of faith" is our trust in God, 5) "the helmet of salvation" is the protection God gives us as His children, through the blood of Christ that cleanses us from sin and through the mind of Christ God is giving us through His Word, 6) "the sword of the Spirit" is the spoken Word of God applied to every situation of our lives, to the lives of those for whom we pray, and to life, and 7) "all prayer" is prayer with the mind and in the Holy Spirit, all of which gives us great confidence, that is, great faith, in God!

- **Note in Ephesians 6:10—19 that "above all," we should "take the shield of faith," for it is our trust in God that allows Him to work! We put on faith by putting on the whole armor of God and praying with <u>all</u> prayer (this includes worship, adoration, confession, thanksgiving, praise, asking for ourselves (supplication), binding, loosing, declaring and decreeing with the Lord's authority, praying with the mind and in the Holy Spirit (tongues), persevering in faith, and asking for others (supplication), especially that they will be bold in speaking the gospel This was like what Jehoshaphat, his praisers and his army did in positioning themselves in faith before the enemy! Doing this will invite God to fight our battles and give us the victory!**

DELIVERANCE AND BLESSING

Repentance, as we say today, "gets a bad rap." It may be seen as too simple, even boring; something we can do before God quickly or even bypass. It may also be seen as embarrassing, and to be avoided, especially when it involves having to make things right with others. This is what Satan wants us to believe! To God, our repentance, personally, as the body of Christ, as a nation and world, for departing from the principles of His Word, is life-changing and life-giving! It opens doors we can walk through for change in our relationship with Him, in our relationships with others, in the Church, in America and the world! It allows for His grace (His undeserved favor) to bring us deliverance and blessing, both here on earth and eternally! To us, to His people, to America and the world, God wants to give "a future and a hope!" It starts as we "call upon Him" and "pray" in repentance. He says to us, to the Church, to America, and the world, what He said to ancient Judah:

"For I know the thoughts that I think toward you, says the Lord, thoughts of peace and not of evil, to give you a future and a hope. Then you will call upon Me and go and pray to Me, and I will listen to you. And you will seek Me and find Me, when you search for Me with all your heart." (Jeremiah 29:11-13)

- *If you are reading this book, feel as if you are facing the future alone, and have never let Jesus Christ be your Savior, Lord, and Friend; put your trust in Him today! God will forgive you, see you through the trials of this life and give you victory, today, in the future and into eternity! Pray this prayer: "Father God, I repent of my sins. I believe You sent your Son Jesus to pay the penalty for my sins so I wouldn't have to. I accept Him as my Savior and receive Your forgiveness because of Him. I also accept Him as my Lord, and with Your Holy Spirit's help, look forward to loving and obeying Him for what He has done for me. Father, come into my life, along with Your Son Jesus, and live in me through Your Holy Spirit. Help me to face the future as Your beloved son or daughter, with faith that you will take care of me on this earth, bless me, give me victories over sin and Satan, healing and miracles through prayer, take care of me, bless me and others through me, and take me home to heaven when You call me or when Jesus returns. In Jesus' almighty name I pray, Amen."*

If you prayed this prayer, you are now born again! God, not self, is now at the center of your life! As a new creation, you can begin to life a new life!

"Therefore, if anyone is in Christ, he is a new creation; old things have passed away; behold; all things have become new." (2 Corinthians 5:17)

The blood of Jesus has washed away your sins! You are a new-born, forgiven child of God! Feed yourself spiritually by reading your Bible daily, strengthening yourself through fellowship with other Christians, accessing Christian media, and when it is possible to do so again, regularly attending a good Bible-believing, Christ-honoring Church. Until then, fellowship with Christians in your family at home and with other Christians, when you can't personally, by phone or social media. Forgive others. God requires it and will give you the grace to do so! Jesus says:

- **"For if you forgive men their trespasses, your heavenly Father will also forgive you. But if you do not forgive men their trespasses, neither will your Father forgive your trespasses." (Matthew 6:14, 15)**

As you surrender to God, He will transform your life! Live every day knowing you are in God's care, and that as His son or daughter, God allows you to pray with authority in Jesus' name! Be repentant, pray for repentance and revival in the Body of Christ and for a Third Great Awakening to come by the power of God's Holy Spirit, bringing many to faith in Jesus Christ and salvation in America and worldwide!

Tell others about your how your sins were forgiven through Jesus Christ, that God will give His people victory in all they face as they trust in Him, and that through Jesus, they too can experience God's love, forgiveness, abundant and transformed life, escape hell and have God's great gift of eternal life!

"I have come that they may have life, and that they may have it more abundantly." (John 10:10b, c)

Jesus died for you! He now lives within you! He is always ready to forgive you and be your Friend! He loves you! He will be with you every day, and one day welcome you to heaven forever!

MONTHLY UNITED PRAYER IN SANTA FE FOR REVIVAL AND AWAKENING BY THE BODY OF CHRIST

(7:00-8:15 p.m. Order of Service) *

I.   Welcome and Opening Prayer by Host Pastor (1-2 min.)

II.   Descriptions of Revival and Awakening, Origin and Importance of United Prayer Meetings, News and/or Events Regarding Prayer for Revival in Santa Fe, in New Mexico, and for Awakening in the U.S. and the World/ Announcement of Next Host Church/Remarks about the Order of Service, by Prayer Coordinators (10-15 min.)

III.   2-3 Songs or Hymns of Worship, led by or chosen by Host Church (10-15 min.)

IV.   Prayer for Revival and Awakening in Santa Fe, New Mexico, the U.S. and the World, in Groups of Three (20 min.)

V.   Corporate Prayer for Revival and Awakening, by individuals who spontaneously pray from Whole Group (20 min.) * **There is prayer guidance on the back of this sheet.**

VI.   Closing Prayer(s), by Prayer Coordinator(s) (1-4 min.)

VII. Closing Words, and Blessing by Host Pastor (1 min.) (Approximately 1 Hr. and 15 Minutes Maximum Time for Meeting)

VIII. Optional Afterglow/At Discretion of Host Church (30 min.)

- Those who would like to stay and continue praying for Revival, Awakening, family, salvation, salvation of friends, healing, special requests, personal concerns, or to give brief testimonies to answered prayer, can stay to pray individually, in small groups or as a whole group, or give brief testimonies.

- Those who choose to stay to fellowship, please do so in another part of the building or outside, to avoid interrupting those who continue praying. (After 30 min., unless given permission by hosts, everyone please vacate the building, so hosts can lock up and go home.)

* **No child care is available. Children may participate,** but if you bring a child and if he or she requires attention, please accompany your child to another part of the building, to the restroom, or outside. Please keep your child beside you during the meeting. Do not leave him or her unsupervised during the meeting.

* 1. If you would like guidance in your praying, you can pray the following Scriptures or related Scriptures you may know, as you are led:

-2 Chronicles 7:14 If My people, who are called by My Name will humble themselves and pray and seek my face and turn from their wicked ways, then will I hear from heaven, forgive their sin and heal their land.

-Jeremiah 18:7-10 The instant I speak concerning a nation and concerning a kingdom, to pluck up, to pull down, and to destroy it, if that nation against whom I have spoken turns from its evil, I will relent of the disaster that I thought to bring upon it. And the instant I speak concerning a nation and a kingdom, to build and to plant it, if it does evil in My sight so that it does not obey My voice, then I will relent concerning the good with which I said I would benefit it.

-Jeremiah 32:17 Ah Lord God, Thou hast made the heavens and the earth by Thy great power and outstretched arm. Nothing is too difficult for Thee!

-Jeremiah 33:3 Call unto Me, and I will answer you, and show you great and mighty things which you know not!

-Habakkuk 3:2 O Lord, I have heard Your speech and was afraid. O Lord, revive Your work in the midst of the years! In wrath remember mercy.

-Joel 2:28-29 And it shall come to pass afterward that I will pour out My Spirit on all flesh; Your sons and your daughters shall prophesy, your old men shall dream dreams, your young men shall see visions, and also on My menservants and on My maidservants I will pour out My Spirit in those days.

Malachi 4:4-6 Remember the Law of Moses, My servant, which I commanded him in Horeb for all Israel, with the statutes and judgments. Behold, I will send you Elijah the prophet before the coming of the great and dreadful day of the Lord. And he will turn the hearts of the fathers to the children, and the hearts of the children to their fathers, lest I come and strike the earth with a curse.

-Matthew 24:14 And this gospel of the kingdom will be preached in all the world as a witness to all the nations, and then the end will come.**-John 15:5, 7-8** I am the vine, you are the branches. He who abides in Me, and I in him, bears much fruit, for apart from Me you can do nothing. If you abide in Me and My words abide in you, you will ask what you desire and it shall be done for you. By this My Father is glorified, that you bear much fruit; so you will be my disciples.

-John 14:6 Jesus said to him, "I am the way, the truth and the life. No one comes to the Father except through Me."

-Acts 3:19 Repent therefore and be converted, that your sins may be blotted out, so that times of refreshing may come from the presence of the Lord, and that He may send Jesus Christ, who was preached to you before.

-**Acts 4:12** Nor is there salvation in any other, for there is no other Name under heaven given among men by which we must be saved.

-**James 5:7, 16,18** Therefore be patient, brethren, until the coming of the Lord. See how the farmer waits for the precious fruit of the earth, waiting patiently for it until it receives the early and latter rain. Elijah was a man with a nature like ours, and he prayed earnestly that it would not rain, and it did not rain on the land for three years and six months. And he prayed again, and the heaven gave rain, and the earth produced its fruit.

*2. Pray Revival for The Church and its leaders in Santa Fe, New Mexico, and in the U.S. Revive us again! Pray for our Government at all levels and its leadership. Pray also for the First Nations.

*3. Pray for Israel: Genesis 12:4 I will bless those who bless you, and I will curse him who curses you; and in you all the families of the earth shall be blessed. **Romans 11:25-27** For I do not desire, brethren, that you should be ignorant of this mystery, lest you should be wise in your own opinion, that blindness in part has happened to Israel until the fulness of the Gentiles has come in. And so all Israel will be saved, as it is written: "The Deliverer will come out of Zion, and He will turn away ungodliness from Jacob; for this is My covenant with them, when I take away their sins."

*4. You may also pray for Revival, Awakening and Transformation in the 7 Mountains of Society, in Santa Fe, in New Mexico, the United States and the World **(Religion, Family, Education, Government, Media, Arts and Entertainment, and**

Business), praying especially that people in each sphere of influence would be convicted of sin by the Holy Spirit, repent of their sins and be saved through or recommit their lives to Jesus Christ and live in or renew their allegiance to His Lordship.* **Praying for Revival and Awakening of souls has Historical Precedent** as **the Moravians**, a German Christian community, began **a continuous prayer watch in 1727, 24 hours a day, for 100 years** and made a great spiritual impact by sending missionaries and renewal workers worldwide before **The 1ˢᵗ Great Awakening,** which swept through Britain and America in the 1730s and 1740s; John and Charles Wesley and George Whitfield began a Bible study and prayer groups in Britain to pray for revival and churches in the colonies joined in united prayer; in 1806 **The Haystack Prayer Meeting** at Williams College in Massachusetts began the modern missionary movement; **In 2ⁿᵈ Great Awakening,** 1800-1840, interdenominational prayer and camp meetings were begun on the American Midsouth frontier, led by preaching evangelists like Timothy Dwight, Peter Cartwright and Charles Finney, and resulted in many salvations and in reforms in American society; **Before the Civil War,** in the late 1850s, a prayer group was started by Jeremiah Lanphier in New York City that spread as a united prayer movement nationwide, bringing revival; before the great **Azusa Street Revival**, which spread worldwide and added 750 million to the Church, there was united prayer for decades, and through the efforts of Frank Bartleman and William Seymour in Los Angeles, brought the revival; **Today,** many churches, many prayer groups, Lou Engle and many other prayer leaders have been praying locally, in our state, the nation and worldwide for revival in the Church and for a **3ʳᵈ Great Awakening!**

* **If you are interested in joining the Prayer Coordinators Team for United Prayer in Santa Fe, to seek to involve your church, and to plan other prayer events, please speak with a Prayer Coordinator immediately after the service.**

ENDNOTES

1   The Cross and the Switchblade, David Wilkerson with John and Elizabeth Sherrill, Random House, 1963. "The Cross and the Switchblade," the film, 1970, starring Pat Boone as David Wilkerson and Erik Estrada as Nicky Cruz, QED Productions, produced by Ken Curtis, Don Harris and Dick Ross, directed by Dan Murray.

2   David Wilkerson's prophecy is quoted from "Friends of Zion, Magazine of the Jerusalem Prayer Team International," "A Divine Interruption," pg. 5, article by Dr. Michael D. Evans, Publisher and Editorial Director, Dr. Michael D. Evans, May 2020.

3   A Great Awakening is Coming, Michael D. Evans, Time Worthy Books, 2020.

4   From "Friends of Zion, Magazine of the Jerusalem Prayer Team International," "A Divine Interruption," article by Dr. Michael D. Evans, Publisher and Editorial Director, Dr. Michael D. Evans, May 2020.

5   Cited from DVD of "Summer of Glory Conference," June 20-23, 2019, David Herzog Ministries, speaker, Lou Engle.

6   America's God and Country Encyclopedia of Quotations, William J. Federer, pgs. 11, 12, AMERISEARCH, INC., St. Louis, MO, 2000.

7   From website americanyawp.com, "John Winthrop Dreams of a City on a Hill, 1630," referring to a sermon preached in 1639 by Puritan pilgrim leader John Winthrop, upon embarking for the "New World" with fellow pilgrims on the ship Arbella.

8   The Cure of All Ills, Mary Stuart Relfe, League of Prayer Inc., 2000. First published in 1988.

9   United States History: Reconstruction to the Present, Prentice Hall, Copyright 2012, by Pearson Education, Inc., pg. 40.

10 "Summer of Glory Conference," June 20-23, 2019, Phoenix/Tempe, AZ, David Herzog Ministries.

11 Azusa Street: An Eyewitness Account, Frank Bartleman, Bridge-Logos, Alachua, Florida, 1980. First published in 1925.

12 Cited from DVD of "Summer of Glory Conference," June 20-23, 2019, Phoenix/Tempe, AZ, David Herzog Ministries, speaker, Lou Engle.

13 Cited from DVD of "Summer of Glory Conference," June 20-23, 2019, Phoenix/Tempe, AZ, David Herzog Ministries, speaker, Lou Engle.

14 Cited from DVD of "Summer of Glory Conference," June 20-23, 2019, Phoenix/Tempe, AZ, David Herzog Ministries, speaker, Lou Engle.

15 The Evangelization of the World in this Generation, Trieste Publishing, 2017. First published by The Student Volunteer Movement, 1900.

16 Cited from DVD of "Summer of Glory Conference," June 20-23, 2019, Phoenix/Tempe, AZ, David Herzog Ministries, speaker, Lou Engle.

17 Cited from DVD of "Summer of Glory Conference," June 20-23, 2019, Phoenix/Tempe, AZ, David Herzog Ministries, speaker, David Herzog.

18 https://www.facebook.com/ShawnBolz/posts about Bob Jones' prophecy.

19 https://www.facebook.com/ShawnBolz/posts about Bob Jones' prophecy.

20 amazon.com/Chiefs-Super-Bowl-Wins-1970-2020, Sports Illustrated magazine covers.

21 <u>Releasing the Prophetic Destiny of a Nation</u>, pg. 322, Dutch Sheets and Chuck D. Pierce, Destiny Image Publishers, Inc., Shippensburg, PA, 2005.

22 From 52 Prayer Points for the State of New Mexico, Walking in Dominion Ministries.wordpress.com, Dec. 4, 2010.

23 "Word of Revival for Santa Fe, NM," from Bernie and Teresa Kuchta, Maryland, U.S.A.

24 Cited from DVD of "Summer of Glory Conference," June 20-23, 2019, David Herzog Ministries, speaker, Lou Engle.

25 Maria Randolph Hanley, photographic art work, "Santa Fe, City of Holy Faith, Jude 20-25."

26 <u>Releasing the Prophetic Destiny of a Nation</u>, Dutch Sheets and Chuck D. Pierce, Destiny Image Publishers, Inc., Shippensburg, PA, 2005.

27 This portion of David Wilkerson's prophecy is quoted from "Friends of Zion, Magazine of the Jerusalem Prayer Team International," "A Divine Interruption," article by Dr. Michael D. Evans, Publisher and Editorial Director, Dr. Michael D. Evans, May 2020.

28 <u>Pioneering Prophetic Patterns of Purpose: When Encountering God Leads to Another Encounter</u>, Dr. Caleb Cooper, Hunter Entertainment Network, Colorado Springs, CO, 2020.

29 <u>Jesus Focused: Awakening Endtime Prophetic Strategy</u>, Dr. Caleb Cooper, Hunter Entertainment Network, Colorado Springs, CO, 2020.

30 Cited from DVD of "Summer of Glory Conference," June 20-23, 2019, Phoenix/Tempe, AZ, David Herzog Ministries, speaker, Lou Engle.

31   <u>The Meal that Heals: Enjoying Intimate, Daily Communion with God</u>, Perry Stone, Charisma Media, 2008.

32   <u>Psalm 91</u>, Peggy Joyce Ruth, Angelia Ruth Schum, Charisma House, 2010.

33   For the amazing effects of the Welsh Revival, see <u>http://truthinhistory.org/the-welsh-revival-of-1904-1905-2.html.</u>

34   This portion of David Wilkerson's prophecy is quoted from "Friends of Zion, Magazine of the Jerusalem Prayer Team International," "A Divine Interruption," article by Dr. Michael D. Evans, Publisher and Editorial Director, Dr. Michael D. Evans, May 2020.

NOTES

NOTES

NOTES

NOTES

NOTES

NOTES

NOTES

NOTES

NOTES

ABOUT THE AUTHOR

Pastor Daniel Castillo, along with his wife Yvonne, are Assistant Pastors at Fruit of the Spirit Ministries, an independent Pentecostal Church pastored by Pastor Dennis and Apostle Eva Gonzales. A graduate of Fuller Theological Seminary, Pasadena, CA, and the Vineyard Leadership Institute, Columbus Vineyard, Columbus, OH, he has been a Presbyterian pastor, and along with his wife Yvonne, Foursquare and independent Pentecostal pastors. For 32 years, he has also been a public and Christian high school teacher, now retired, having taught U.S. Government, History and Spanish.

You can contact Pastor Castillo at dcastillo54@yahoo.com